Broken

A True Story

Written by
Lateisha Varner

Atlanta, GA

Copyright © 2011 by Lateisha Varner
All rights reserved.
No part of this book may be reproduced in any form without written permission from the publisher.

ISBN: 1-930231-40-7 / 978-1-930231-40-5

Editor: Elfriede Kelly Johnson
Book Design and Layout: The Rod Hollimon Company

This book is based on true events of the life of the Author. Names and locations have been changed to protect the privacy and freedom of those whose paths she may have crossed.

Printed in the USA
First Edition

Encouragement

As you enter into my world, you will notice that I will be jumping from story to story. That's how my life was. I had a lot of different things going on, but it all made me a strong and independent woman. My life and the challenges that I faced wasn't a game to me. It was a test. I wanted to cry each and every day, but I couldn't because now I had kids who needed me. So you see my life became harder and harder to deal with. I had much to bear.

Dealing with my problems made me write poems. I had a bad attitude during that time. I was writing only because I was thinking of all the people who had done me wrong. I now look at life as a big challenging world. You never know what your test will be. For those who are going through the same problems, look at your life as an almost dying flower, when you pour water on it, it will rise again. No matter what life may have in store for us, never forget there is only one person in this world who makes the final decision. There have been plenty of times when I thought no one cared, and the strangest thing to me was how I was making it through. Each time I was at my lowest, I got on my knees and ended up back on my feet. From my experiences, I know that you are never alone. Just hold on and have faith. It won't be easy so don't give up. Trust me, there is someone out there praying for you. Please don't let your problems take over, grow from them. Remember, this book is about who I once was. It's not who I am now. It was written just because of my pain. I hope you enjoy my book.

Acknowledgement

To my four boys; Jaquavious, Gerald, Jarmonte, Jr., and Justice, I want you guys to know that I will always love you. I will never turn my back on you. To my Mom, Vivian, I know we have been through a lot since the divorce of you and my dad. Mom, let's prayerfully put our differences behind us and move forward together. I love you Mom.

To the man I prayed for, of course you are the true love of my life, and without you I don't think I would have made it this far. So let's grow up and old together like we promised. I love you baby.

To my twin sister Lakeisha, I want to thank you for listening and understanding me through all of my hard times. Thank you for not turning your back on me even - when I made it impossible to deal with me.

To my sister, Demetress, I want to thank you for keeping a smile on my face with all those silly ass jokes you tell during the times I needed to be uplifted.

To my sister, Andrea, I want to thank you for being kind and sweet.

To my brother, Oliver, I want you to know that you are my heart and my only brother on mom's side of the family. Bro keep your head up high because that's the direction we're headed.

To the man that made me a Believer and a Trooper, my dad Oliver, Sr. I can't express what I want to say about you because you are a million words in one. Dad you are my pal and I love you for being you. I told you that I was going to make all of this possible sooner or later and I did.

To my little sister, Laquita, by another mother, I want you to know that I love you sweetie.

To my little twin brothers Marquise and Jarquise, by another mother, I really didn't have a chance to know you both, but I want you to know that your big sister has always loved you.

To my friend Shalethia, when we met we became close friends. We were more like sisters than friends. We had many crazy times together. I miss the friendship.

To my best friends Jazz, April, and Carlin, girl's I thank God for you all. Mostly, because when no one would listen to me, you all did. Y'all didn't care if it was 4am in the morning. Even though we all were going through the same thing at that time, I know we have been a blessing to each other and I thank God for placing you three in my life.

Elfriede Johnson, you have been more than a friend, stepmother, and Manager. I don't know if I ever had the chance to say thank you. But I do thank you. As a former employee, you inspired me to believe that I could break through any obstacle as long as I didn't try to handle them on my own and just give them to God instead. Look at me now, again I say, thank you.

To my mother- in- law Donna, I thank God for giving my kids a chance to bond with you, and bringing our family closer. I love you.

To Gilda, my son's Auntie on his dad's side of the family, you know I love you. You also play a big part in my life. Thank you and keep doing a good job. You know what I mean.

To my son's grand dad, Gerald Sr., who is going through his challenges, may God place you back on your feet very soon. Your grandson and I thank God for placing you in his life. We love you so much for that, and for playing the role we wish his dad, Gerald Jr. could have played. Again, I thank you.

Now, to my other close friend, Bossie, I love you, and thank you for being a friend in times of need.

If I forgot anyone, I didn't mean to. I also thank and love you too.

Lateisha C. Varner

Contents

1. The End | 7

2. Growing Up | 11

3. Mom's Affair | 18

4. We Had to Move | 30

5. My First Love: Toney | 50

6. My Second Love: Joe | 60

7. The Man I Prayed For | 77

8. My Kids | 85

9. Allowing God to Take Over | 89

Part 1: The End

21 years since the accident. I came to realize that this all wasn't based on John and my mom. It was based on the people they hurt. I'm now sitting in front of the church attending John's funeral. To sit here and watch the tears fall from his kids and wife's eyes. Let me not forget to say mine and my sister's also. I can see the pain and regret in my mom's eyes too. My mom and John were young when all this occurred. I feel sorry that it happened, but no one can stand in the way of God's work. They hurt us and this isn't fair. What are we to do now? Live? No, I don't think so. Justice to me has not been served until someone tells us why. John can't so that leaves it all to my mom. She can't because there are always two sides to a story.

Now that I'm grown, let me end it at this: May god forgive you both and give me the strength to move on from this. And I pray that I don't follow her footsteps, even though I do have her genes. Because this is very sad, life is taking me on a long journey. Why? I don't know, but what I can say is that I have seen and been through so much.

At the time my childhood was taken, I was about ten years old. I'm now thirty three and still asking that same question - why? It really doesn't matter anymore. I will never get the truth. I guess it's not for me to know.

I can respect God's work so I'm going to stop blaming and let his will be done. This is the end of my childhood. It's now time for me to grow.

Why Wonder

Sometimes I wonder a lot
People say it's not a good thing to do
But I learned for myself
Not to pay the devil any attention.
I go to GOD in a bright room and I ask him
To help me through this battle,
I can't face him, I can't hear him,
But I can feel the warmth of his spirit down in my soul.
No more wondering he revealed.
I'm the GOD that is never far.
I'm the GOD that's always in your heart.

Smile

Look in the mirror what do you see?
Touch your skin what do you feel?
Is what you see is it your life?
Is what you feel is it real?
GOD placed you here for a reason
He can handle all your trials
So tell me
When you see whatever you see
When you feel what you feel
Knowing that GOD can handle all trials
Doesn't that give you more reasons to smile?

Lateisha Varner

Who wants to know?

So I get my pin and start to write
Is that wrong or is it what makes me strong
Wondering what lies on my paper
I wish like hell they even might
What's my name, what's my age, where I'm from?
I thought now days all it took
Was the print from my thumb
Sitting here not knowing what to say
Now they're looking directly in my face
Praying the lord will get me out this place
Oh, just ask who wants to know
Who wants to know isn't for everyone
It's for those with the other pin
Trying to see if they can find what lies within
I speak loud, I write with pride
My dignity is all I have lift inside
Can't care what white or black
Woman or man don't care to hear what I'm saying
But here is where its stops
I rise tall and take whatever stands
 I'm proud to be a black woman

Listen
I'm going to stay me, continue to do what I do best
And let no one ever make me feel low
That's why I always ask
Who wants to know?

Part 2: Growing Up

As a little girl, growing up was exciting. I grew up with three sisters and one brother. At this time, my mom and dad were blissfully married. As a family, we always went out to have family times together. Either we would go to the movies or out to eat. My dad had a good job working for a company called Lock Smith that supported his family. I used to wait at the front door on my dad to get home from work only to jump in his arms and hear him call me his little Princess. I was always told that I looked the splitting image of my dad.

My mom was a stay home mom. My dad was the kind of man that thought a woman shouldn't have to work if she had a man living with her, and that the man should be the one getting dirty.

I loved my family so dearly. They were all I had growing up. My siblings and I were very close. When you saw one you also would see the others. We grew up in a church going home. I always waited on Sundays to come. I was in the choir. The name of my church going home was called LWC of God in Christ. My church was a big church. It was a family church. My mom's mother was a member first and then she invited my family. We have been members of LWC of God in Christ every since.

One day at church, this lady named Ms. Betty was all in my ear. She was known as the mean lady of the church. She was also known as the *Holy Ghost Lady* to all the kids at my church. Ms. Betty yelled so loud in my ear (thank you Jesus, Glory to God) I thought that she was going to die very soon. Only because she was called the Holy Ghost Lady, I was afraid of her. I didn't think I was ready to see her Ghost yet. I didn't know too much about church yet like the other kids, but I never heard anyone say that the Holy Ghost wasn't going to really be a Ghost. I can't believe that I waited years to see Ms. Betty turn all white one day like Casper the Friendly Ghost. I'm glad that I learned more about church because I got tired of waiting on Ms. Betty's Ghost.

You know I saw that sometimes, even though you go to church, that didn't mean you would be happy or a glorious person after leaving. At times, I would see my dad looking sad or maybe my mom. I didn't let that distract me. I continued to be a child, while my mom and dad continued to pretend that they both were happy.

"You two need to go back in and get prayer," Grand momma said to my parents.

"Come here Teasey" my grand momma said to me, "let me bite your cheeks."

I asked, "Grand momma, why do you keep calling me Teasey?"

"Cause baby you are your grand momma's Teasey Weesey."

"Hey Grand momma?"

"What baby?" replied Grand Momma.

"God told me yesterday that I was going to be a writer." *I excitedly said.*

"Did he sweetie?" grand momma asked.

"Yep, and he said that he wanted me to be a poet. I wrote my first poem when you went into the hospital the last time, and I thought that you were going to die on me. I also named the poem after you and it's called "Grand Mom," do you want to hear it Grand momma?" I asked.

Grand Mom

Grand mom please don't leave me
You are my one and only friend
If you close your eyes that will all end
I thought I was your Teasey Weesey
Who then will bite my cheeks?
Please tell God I need you? Not to take you today
Cause I want to continue this smile on my face.

"Did you like that Grand momma?" I asked.

"I loved that Teasey. Baby you don't have to worry I'm not going nowhere" she said. My grand momma then gave me a hug and it felt sooo good. Every time she hugged me I felt like I was being wrapped in a baby blanket.

"Everybody have a safe and blessed day. I will see all of you Wednesday night," the preacher said to us. My mom and dad took us out to eat because my mom said she wasn't in the mood to cook. When we all got back home my mom and dad still looked as if they were having problems.

I just couldn't figure out what was going on with the two of them. Trying to pretend like nothing was going on, I decided to go outside with my siblings. When we came back into the house, I decided to write a poem on my siblings.

Siblings

It's four of you and I tell GOD everyday thank you
For allowing me to be raised with people that's so true
We play together, we eat together, and we sleep together
There's nothing else I could ask for
While we take our trip through this stormy weather

Grandmother

I thought I knew, I thought it was a dream,
Until my eyes opened and it was you.
Couldn't see you in that bed,
Knowing you was half lifeless.
Got my hands placed on your soft head.
A lot to say that couldn't be said.
I didn't want to accept the fact that it was you
 Knowing losing you would make my life blue.
Your face had such a glow,
Your voice was so soft spoken,
I wish I could've stayed asleep.
It would've been one less loss,
Can I accept being without such a person?
One that gave me much love,
One that sheltered me
One that covered me when I was asleep,
I wish I didn't have to awake to this misery.
So I prayed each day wasn't your day,
But yet, time has taken you so far away.
Now that I'm awake, I have come to realize, that day was your day.

To You

When looking in your eyes
Seems to always catch me by surprise
I find myself thanking God
For placing someone like you in my life;
True friends are hard to find,
So many have made me blind,
But you are the one who never left me crying.

My butterfly friend

Who is he or she? Just staring at me
Who sent it? What does it want
This butterfly must know me
Does it not have a Mother
What about a sister or brother
Something of its own kind
I don't understand what could be
On this butterfly's mind
It acts as if it understands what I'm saying
Not only does my paper listen to me
But this butterfly has some interest also
Will it go with me to the end?
I'm not sure
But I do know I now have a
Butterfly friend

This is a picture of my loving
Grandmom (to the left) Sara Stone.
May she rest in peace

Part 3: Mom's Affair

As a child, I didn't know much about grown folks business because my mom and dad always told me and my siblings to always stay in a child's place. So we did as our parents commanded us to do. When mom and dad wanted their time to talk, they would send me and my siblings outside to play for a while. August 16, 1988 is a day I will never forget. My dad and I were sitting on the front porch of our house. My dad was putting three ugly pony tails in my head, preparing me and my sibling for school.

During this time, it had been about two days since my mom hadn't been home. Where was she? I wasn't sure... All I knew is my dad was very sad. I sat beside him asking if he was okay. I wasn't used to seeing my dad ever being so sad.

"I'm fine baby," he said sadly, "I'm just hoping nothing bad happened to your mom. Okay, Teisha, I'm done with your hair and it's time for you and the others to leave for school."

"Bye daddy," we all yelled out loud while getting on the school bus. I didn't want to leave my dad, but I needed my education, and I was too young to understand what he was going through anyway.

It was now 3:15pm and school was letting out. Getting off the school bus, daddy wasn't waiting for us on the porch. He was in the house preparing dinner. Something that mom was supposed to be doing. My dad was not used to doing what mom used to do. I could tell from his movements. He and my mom

Broken

were high school lovers. Where ever my mom was she was tearing my dad down by not being home.

It was now 6:23pm. I heard a knock at the door.

"It's now time for you to leave." I could hear those words traveling upstairs through the hall way where I was standing so I ran down stairs and it was my mom. I was very happy to see her; but when I got down there it was my mom with a tall light skinned man. He was very good looking. I thought maybe he was the insurance man, or maybe a friend of the family.

My dad was half way out the door.

"Dad where are you going?"

"Babygirl, your mom and I are going to be apart for a while."

"No daddy! Stay here with me, please don't go," I said sadly.

"Babygirl, I'll be back tomorrow to get my clothes, I'll see you then."

"Okay daddy."

"Fat where you at?," this man yelled out to my twin sister.

"Here I come John," my sister answered back.

When my sister got downstairs, this man asked if she wanted to go with him to the corner store. Of course, my sister said yes. So happily I said, "Me too? Can I go with you too?"

By now, I know that his name is John. But anyway, he said to me, "not you Common Sense."

Now this man came in my house, ran my dad away, and behind that he had the nerve to call my daddy's little princess Common Sense.

This man got so used to calling me Common Sense in just one day. Each time I had to pass him in the house he would either say, come here Common Sense, Do this Common Sense, your mother this Common Sense. If I was old enough I would have stood outside of a child's place, and said, "first of all you don't know shit about me. So keep those weak ass comments to yourself. And that my dad and GOD had already told me that I was going to have plenty of sense just wait and see."

Maybe John should have used his Common Sense not to come into another man's house like he was the big bad wolf. He was better off playing Captain Save a... What kind of man will respect a woman who would let another man talk to her child like that? Only a desperate one.

I should have told him to use his Common Sense and leave our house. I started thinking, "what has Mom told this man about me for him not to like me. Did she hate me that much to allow such a thing." Now that John and my sister are back, I was waiting to see what John bought her at the store. She had something alright, but not enough to share with the rest of us. I wasn't mad at my sister, I was mad at John and my mom.

The next day, I'm ready to see my dad, but when my dad came, John did not want my dad to come in the house. My dad pushed his way in so that he could get his things and go. But instead, John took it upon himself and hit my dad in the head with his gun.

"Why did you do that Stupid? This is my dad."
"Stay in a child's place princess," my dad said to me. "Baby I'm okay."

My mom asked my dad to leave again. At this time, my brother and sisters heard the commotion and ran down stairs. My dad was getting into his car. John ran up to my dad and hit him again. After that, my dad got his gun stood in front of John and then shot him. My dad was arrested, but he was let out for self defense cause he and my mom were still married. This was still my dad's house that John brought his drama to.

John ended up paralyzed because when my dad shot him the bullet entered his spine. Now I wonder what does my mom have to say about herself, and what she put my dad and her kids through. Now I don't know how long my mom and John had been dating and it really didn't matter anymore…my dad was gone. I did not like John at all after that. My mom gave him too much attention. Not only that, John seemed to love only one of mom's kids and she had five in all. All I could say was that John stole my mom from my dad, and that motherly love from me that my mom promised me. My mom made me feel like an unwanted child after John came into our lives. He saw that I didn't like him, but he didn't care because he already had my mom, and she had showed him that he came before me.

After all the commotion died down, I found out that my mom and John had been dating for a while. "What?" I said to myself, "this man now owes me his life because he had just taken mine." Now that I'm older and I can say and do as I please, let it be said clearly: Fuck the both of you for playing with my life. And I hope that both of you drown in your thoughts wondering where did I get my Common Sense.

Common Since

Does that mean you are confused
Does that mean you are loose
Does that mean you won't make it?
      Or
Can it mean you are not confused
Can it mean you'll never be loose
Or maybe it means I will make it
Those two words have followed me all my life
Not you or no one else saw that
It went so deep inside me
Here and then I had not one bit of sleep
I tried doing what I was raised to do
      Pray
At the time that didn't help
I guess I got on my knees too late
See the sun never shine directly on me
I don't see why not? I did pray to be burned
And put out of my miseries
Again I did what I was raised to do
      Pray
Still that didn't work, where is he
I know he has to have time for me
God did make him master over my disaster
I hope this don't last forever.

Them

You see at the beginning I had little trust
Because everyone around me had the smell of fake lust
I looked at them as the walking dead, saying in my head
Ashes, to ashes, dust to dust
So tell me who was I to trust?
Someone whispered in my ears
Seek yee first and you shall have eternal life
Yeah right I said
Why then everybody around me smell half dead
They stank I can't stand them
I wish they all would redeem
But that's too much like a child's dream
Always wishing upon a star
Just waiting to see one fly down from the sky above
I'll just keep dreaming
Because down here there'll never be true love

Lateisha Varner

Mother

Mother you will always be acknowledged...
I don't think I could've made it without you.
You shielded me for many years,
In your presence I've always felt safe,
I knew of nothing but your loving face.

I can't imagine what it was like to bare me;
That goes to show how much you cared for me.
Roses and candy can't make up for all you have done;
You brought me here on that day called my birthday.
After carrying me nine months into this wonderful place,
I want you to know, you should always have it your way.

God must have had so much favor over you.
They say where there is a child there is a home.
You must have had peace and strength to carry me;
Just waiting for me to be close and near you,
To hold me, to love me, and to protect me...

Whatever your unknown reasons were,
They are the reasons for me to say
Every day is your day.

The Unsaid

Talk about it but it can't be explained,
Family and friends wondering if I'm insane
Feel my pulse to see if I'm alive.
It's my vision and I'm tired of it making me feel as if I'm dying.
Looking for an ear someone that can hear
Open my mouth not yet ready for it to come out.
Daytime, all are around, hello, by, see you later
Still not a sound;
Night time has arrived, I'm tired, go to sleep.
Still it's me, left with the unsaid.

Mom

Mom you are my shining star
Not no one else, I don't care who they are
You babied me when I cried
You covered me when I was cold
One to two you have to clue
How much I thank god for choosin' you
To be my Guidant, and care taker
If I had to choose again
I don't think I would find no one greater
Mother you played your part
And that I will never forget
So on this day It's my joy to say – –

Who Am I

Was not here to last, gained a couple of back stabbers
Kept my head high, in just a moment their going to cut your butt
Like the grass on my lawn
Hanging around but no one notice
Keep moving along or just sing that same old sad song
Haven't figure me out yet
But they call you the smartest and I'm the retardest
You're the honest, I'm the dumbest
Again keep moving along
Or just sing that same old sad song
How about I rose while holding my head high
Singing that same old sad song
Holding that same old bag
Knowing this is my living past.

Lateisha Varner

Life

It's easy to deal with and I'm proud to be here
I love walking down my street thinking of no one but me
Talking to god that man that died on Calvary just for thee
Wondering if he would answer my thoughts
The thoughts I know gone make a change in me
Clearing all those that's not of him, far away from me
I want to enjoy this place while I can
It took such to build this wonderful place
That's why I can't see myself astray
Evil is all around me but there's nothing I have to fear
God I trust and I will 'til my dying day
Life has surprises for me each and everyday
My test, I will never know which one I have to face
I fear no man but yet its man that's trying to take me down
I know he is near, I place my life in his hands, and then say amen.

Father

It had to be hard to take on me,
Better said your responsibility
You never left me instead you gave
Your love and care
All I was able to give was a da, da, goe, goe
You showed that was more than enough for you
Everything looked so clear and blue
Each time I stared at you.
From the look in your eyes,
And the touch of your hands,
I sense that I would always be in safe hands
Looking at you trying to hold me
You did your best,
That was a funny site to see
Showing off for little ole me.
I'm glad that God chose you to be my dad
And I wouldn't trade you if I had.
I will never forget you staying with me
And not running astray.
So I just want to say that each and every day
Will always be your day.

Part 4: We Had To Move

My Dad never did get his things from the house that night of the shooting. He came back three weeks later for his things. That day, my Dad asked my siblings and I to go outside to play for a while, and that he needed to talk with our mom. Before going outside, I asked my dad why we have to move? He said because your mom couldn't leave the projects. Years later, I understood the saying: you can take the girl from the project, but you can't take the projects out the girl. In my mind, I was thinking the conversation was going to be on working their problems out. Outside of the house, I could hear Mom and Dad arguing like crazy. Being a child, I didn't care to hear what the argument was about so my brother and I decided to take a tour to the community playground.

We were loved by all those who surrounded us so we had nothing to be troubled about while being there. Back then, were we were living, everybody was family so we were in good company. My brother and I preferred to go play on the merry-go-round. My brother was eight years old. While he was spinning me around and around, I leaned my head back and I saw a plane going across the sky. Then I started fantasizing about what it would be like being on an airplane. I just wanted to pack my things and fly away. On the other hand, my mom and dad wouldn't get on an airplane if someone paid them all the money in the world so I took that thought out of my head.

It was nothing like going around and around on that merry-go-round while my brother was being the pilot spinning and spinning. Something came over me while I was going around

Broken

in a circle. I resumed the thought of wondering what was going on at home so I asked my brother to continue spinning while he takes me around my so called world. Not knowing when this merry-go-round was going to stop, I was just waiting to place my feet back on this unsafe ground. So I started praying to GOD that when I got home everything would be okay.

I started singing this church song called," shake the Devil off," and in the name of JESUS, I hoped that GOD was going to work things out between my parents and take care of our home.

On my way back home, I saw my Dad leaving out the door with his bags in his hands. I ran as fast as I could to catch up with him before he drove out of my life. When I reached my Dad, I was in tears and I gave him the longest hug that I could give anyone. I was holding onto him for dear life. I didn't want to let go, but my mom was yelling at me to come away from the car. I did as I was told and my Dad drove away.

After my Dad left us, it seemed like I had sold my soul to the Devil. I loved my Dad so much. My Dad was the only one paying me attention. He made me his little princess, and after he left, I felt like the Fairy GOD Child and I started to change.

A couple of months had passed since my Dad left. My mom divorced him eventually. I started running away from home. It was not my decision, but my cousin's. She was about two years younger than me, but much, much faster in life. She was a child who had many issues on her shoulders - much more than I had on mine. I can't even compare my life to hers. She started having kids when she was in the seventh grade. (Talking about where were her parents). I only ran away from home because I didn't want my cousin out there alone. Plus, I didn't think my mom would even notice. I didn't see my face on news.

People treated her so badly and treated me with kindness. I thought by me being with her they would be kind to her too. I can say that GOD did protect me while I was out there. I met a guy who was a friend of my cousin's boyfriend. I want to thank this guy for not taking advantage of me during times we slept next to each other. He didn't know anything about me. He could have looked at me as a runaway whore, but he didn't. I guess GOD showed him different. This guy fed me when I was hungry. He even covered my body like a shield when other females were trying to fight me over him. They didn't know that he and I weren't in a relationship. I should've told them that he was my protector from GOD until my Mom and Dad came for me.

My Mom and Dad had no clue where to find me. This guy went and found them and brought them to me. It was like he knew they didn't know where to start looking. I will always be grateful for this guy for getting me back home. When I got home, my Dad was there. He gave me a tight hug and said I scared him. He told me not to ever do that again and went on his way. He was only there to help find me. On the other hand, it felt like my Mom was not happy to see me. She was not happy that I was back. My Mom and I talked, but I could feel her lack of happiness and I remember how she thought I was having sex. I tried telling her that I wasn't. I wanted to leave again, but I didn't because I was afraid from the last time when I returned.

I watched my Mom everyday for her to never say "I missed you." I so badly wanted to say to her, "Lady you just don't know what the hell I'm going through right now. Woman, mentally, I'm stressed the fuck out. Emotionally sweetie, I'm a helpless child that is seeking love. I miss my Dad, and I need you. Can you just be there for me just *one day?*" But yet and still, I loved her (honor thy Mother and thy Father so the bible says.) I asked GOD over and over again, "What about honoring the child you brought into this world? And for what? Why me?!"

After the divorce, my Mom moved us all to the projects, which is called by another name, "the ghetto." My siblings and I

Broken

didn't want to move from our five bed room home. We were used to the lifestyle of being a whole family with my Dad. But we had no choice but to deal with our new life without our Dad. Moving to the projects became okay. I saw that it was the place where thugs and low income Moms live. Either they didn't have jobs paying much money, or maybe they were just here surviving and trying to make a living until they could do better. Some of them had no choice; they just got used to the government doing all the work for them. Not saying if that's bad or good. For the record, I'm not going to sit here and act like the projects wasn't fun. It became the best time of my life actually. I was young and soon started having fun again. I taught myself just to not grow into this place and accept this life. It just wasn't enough for me.

Going to school close to the projects was torture. Kids who didn't live on my street always seemed to pick on me and my siblings. Once I got to school and went to class, I always started beating my pencil on the school desk and kelp getting in trouble over and over again. I never knew why I didn't even care at that time. All I could say was something was always on my mind, and being young, I knew this wasn't normal.

One thing I did extremely dislike about these projects was seeing small kids playing in the streets without anyone looking after them. Their daddies were shooting craps to buy themselves new clothes, but not care for their little ones. You see, the cops back then weren't all that hard on thugs. I used to think either they were afraid or just didn't care. Now that I'm older, at times, I sit and cry when I look back at what has been given and what has been taken. The truth, growing up was the most horrible part of my life. Family and friends were splitting, dying or going to jail.

Tina and her sister Lisa were the first people we met when we moved to the projects. They came over and introduced themselves to me and my family. We all were in the fourth grade. We became friends with them both from that point on. Tina was a type of female that I had never met before. She was too advanced for me. I really wasn't able to keep up with her. For her to be the age she was at the time we met, I never understood how someone so young could be so fast. "Where was her Mom?" I always said out loud to myself because I wasn't bold enough to ask her. I wanted to be her. She had a lot going on in her life as a child also, but was able to deal with her problems better than me. I saw so much wanting to be loved; love that she needed. I think that's how she and I became the best of friends. We both were searching for the same thing. Fathers and mothers were around but we didn't get much attention from either of them.

    Now to the middle of our friendship, my mom allowed the two of them to spend the night at our place. Tina and I slept together, while her sister and my twin sister slept together. I had the feeling that Lisa was getting very close to me. So each night, I would experience something different from her. Some nights she would just rather kiss. I guess she thought that would make us close. Anyhow, we all went out one night to this club called Chat that and got tow up from the floe up - a ghetto phrase. When we got back home, my twin sister and Tina's sister, Lisa, both gave us all away. They were so drunk. My mom slapped my sister's face so hard and she just stood there like nothing had happened. So I looked at her and started laughing and said," Girl did you not just feel that?" She was so drunk that she didn't even respond to what I had just asked her. She went in the house and went to sleep. I went behind her. Tina and her sister went home, which was across the street from our house.

From that point, I started drinking beer more and more every chance I could. Beer made me fight, beer made me tell my life, it even made me cry. My life was a disaster, but every time I drank

Broken

beer, it made me see who I really was. I was the person that everybody seemed to hate.

Tina and her sister Lisa had to move back to their home town, which was New York. I got a phone call one year later from Lisa telling me that Tina had died in a car wreck. A year and five months later, my sister and I get another phone call from New York saying that Lisa was now dead from a bad car wreck. At that point, I felt really lost. I wanted to drink my life away when I heard the news. The one thing that never left my side during my time of pain and hurt was my note book. I was able to write and tell that notebook everything. It seems funny, kind of strange, but it was real. That notebook never got up to use the restroom, it never told me to hold on so that it can see who's on the phone or at the door, that notebook never told my problem to anyone else until I was ready for my hurt and pain to be known. That notebook moved when I said move. You know what I loved most about my notebook? It never talked back. It just listened.

Now that Tina was gone, I saw that I was becoming so much like her "a thug girl." When that happened, I don't think too many people were messing with me anymore. If they did, they didn't stay in my hood. I had to go through so much to gain respect for me and my sister now that Tina was gone. Tina made sure I didn't back down from anyone and I didn't. I wish I could say how much she was to me because she was everything. She showed and taught me so many things that my mom and dad should have. Not only had that, she showed me things that my mom and dad couldn't share with me also. I loved her at that time. She was the only one showing me what and how to love. She was my lover and soul mate. She always had my back, front, and side.

There was this other person who was also known as my best friend. His name was Fred. I met Fred just a little after I met

Tina and her sister. Fred was the only male friend I ever had and he will always be. He was so funny and loved to tell jokes all the time to keep me smiling. He also liked to dance from time to time for attention, and boy did he get it with them dances he used to come up with. Fred was a happy and sad little boy at the same time. Our friendship ended very fast. He was having problems at home with his family too. His dad was in a relationship with another woman who wasn't his mom. Fred used to tell me that he wasn't being treated right by this woman so I told him that it was okay to come to my house anytime he felt afraid. We played video games to keep from been noticed by our parents. He taught me how to play super Nintendo. Today, that is still the only game that I know how to play. Every time I play that game, I think of Fred and how much fun we had together as friends when Tina wasn't around. We thought that we could protect each other, but we really couldn't. At the age of fourteen, Fred's life was cut short. Fred was drinking beer with a couple of his other friends. They all were drinking beer - knowing it was wrong. They were young and having fun I guess. Their parents would have not found out because those were the kids who no one noticed so why not have a drink. After they were done drinking and playing let's get fucked up together, Fred and his friends decided to visit the public park for a swim - forgetting that they all were drunk. Fred got caught on something at the bottom of the pool. From what I heard, everyone tried to help pull him up, but he was too heavy. I wondered if somewhere in his mind, he looked for me to protect him. I really did miss him, but he was in a better place than I.

Fred was treated so badly down here in this cold, cold ass world. I remember when we both made snow angels in the ground one snowy day outside. After his death, I wish I had taken a picture of our angel; therefore, I would've known I always had an angle near to keep me safe. Fred felt unsafe and unwanted. I think that's why GOD took him so young. Why did he forget me? Did he not want me by his side also? Come back soon, I prayed that prayer every night. God must have other plans; I lay across my bed looking up at the ceiling in my bedroom saying to myself.

Some kids still hated me in the project. Why? I never knew. I guess because I was different from them, or maybe they wished they had a mom like mine. She had become the play mom to every child in the neighborhood. I could've understood that. She was a very nice person, I felt, just not to me. I needed her to be there during the time my dad was gone, but she was too caught up to see that. My mom was my mom. She was not my mother. All the fancy clothes, the food, and the other extras that she did for me, I thank her for it all, but I would've traded it in for her love. I know this may seem a little harsh, but it's the truth. I loved her, but I hated her for not being there.

The Outside

Standing outside it's very late
Brushing against my skin
It's the cool air from the midnight breeze
Shaking to my knees
Now having flashes of my past memory
During my teen years my friends and I
Slept outside plenty of times
With no worries or fear on our minds
So many wanted to hang
I thought it wasn't a good idea
It was better if they took a chill pill
We were just a little too much for whomever
We were joker, we were story teller
Just hanging out enjoying this cool breezy weather
It was amazing once everything got sleepless and quiet
We were able to see and hear it all
To see the plane go across the sky
We made a quote that if one dies
At least we would know how close the other was
To still hear each other cry

Peace

It must be nice to live with it
To experience the joy that it brings
From the burn in my heart, to the smile on my face
I don't know not one person
That wouldn't want to be in my place
Peace comes from within
If you can get past your pain
Forget those that drove you insane
And pray to god that you don't live in vane
Then you would experience the same
Moving forward can be very hard when you're facing challenges
That push close to your heart
But it's up to you to break that chain
So next time if there's a next
You'll be stronger to put out that flame
Look at it this way
A clear mind means less stress
Less stress means you're blessed
Being blessed means you're nothing like thee
And being nothing like thee
Puts you back at peace

Lateisha Varner

I wonder

Have you ever felt happy as ever before?
Have you ever felt life before time?
I know, what such saying but it's mines I speak of
The things I have been through does not compare to yours
God has made me see so much that many wish
I ask was I brought here to bring peace
Do I have a mission that need to be complete?
None can see the person you have made me to be
Only I wish that you could bring all to reality
So easy to see that I'm nothing like thee
Am I in body? But here in flesh, none like the rest
Don't know what's going on, all I know is I'm blessed
My purpose I will never know and don't care
I take this gift and I promise to share
You gave your life for my sake and I thank you so dearly
But can it be that I'm so close and so nearly to you
I feel like we have such a bond
Not that I'm complaining because I'm having fun
You said you will always be there
I wonder is it here that you speak of,
Or can you be talking about heaven above?
It really doesn't matter, because I will always be one of yours

Friendship

Supposedly, I needed you most,
Will you be that friend indeed?
That friend when I cry you cry?
All that can be given is nothing
Like having you by my side
Life has brought us close
Not a soul can change that.
A matter that is all fact
I would like to say thank you for having my back.

Stump

Couldn't move when I heard the news
Had no faith to show me the way
I give my life to you make me whole
Place me where I need to be
If I just hold on and stay strong
It will not last long
Trailer come so past you don't know what hit you
Had no one to help me through
All I could do when I thought of you
Was lift my hand and stump my feet
I want to shout hallelujah praise the lord
My soul belong to you, because when I cry you make it dry
When I couldn't breathe you gave me air
Yes I think my lord for being there
Through my entire trailer I could not bare
So please don't take your love away
I really need you so I would not stray
Others in the world need shown the way
Open arms will lead them there
Bare to them show them you care
Tears drops as the cleanses go through my soul
Think you for making me whole.

Going Home

I know you was with him or her yesterday
But now it's time for him or her to fly away
This life wasn't promised to either of us
But time did say we would all soon pass away
It's okay to cry but remember don't ask why
Even though he or she is gone, their smile, their kindness
But most of all their spirit is a reason to move on and be strong
I know you had a lot to say but time took him or her away
He or she will be going home to our father
So please don't be sad
The flood gates in heaven have opened
Believe it or not they're not the last
Now or later your time will come
Get it right so that he or she can meet you at the thrown
A place where god calls home
So dry those tears and remember the time you spent
With he or she these past years
Because you will see he or she again

You and I

Now that his soul has been set free
Where does that leave you and I
The higher power did say he would be back
That I have read and know it's all a fact
He is not gone from us
He leaves his ashes because his father needed his soul
Set him free he is going to a better
Place than you and I
He is our father and soon will be back.

Sister

*Sister you and I have done so much
When you saw one you saw the other
We have nothing but love for one another
When I cried you cried
I love you for being by my side.*

Young Sta

Remember when we was young
Playing and running around the hood
No playground but it was all good
There was too much love spread in our hood
That's where I'll grab all my memories
So sad to see you go
At least you won't have to worry about
This mess down here anymore
Though time has taken you very fast
leavin' most so sad
Some have not one clue why
In God words he did say
To be absence from the body
Is to be present with the lord
So I will not cry because
This is not our goodbye
Let it be me saying goodnight.

Freedom

Will we ever have peace?
In this world they call the land of free
I always wondered where the liberty was
Cause this place is nowhere near my destiny
We can't even walk down these streets
From all the hateration
I don't know who's out there planning the day for my assassination
Wondering why did they put sirens on a cop's car
They no damn well they aren't trying to save us
We come better off saving ourselves
It's not like I can trust my life in the hands of someone else
Will there ever be peace
Brothers will they one day give up chasing these streets
Setting a trap for themselves to be placed in the penitentiary
What since is that? Cause once you're there
Ain't no turning back, you have just given yourself a number
That will be joining the rest of their stacks
Will there ever be peace
Sisters why are we still having babies with no fathers
Are you not feed up? Just for thirty minutes of lust
Are you not tired of standing in that welfare line?
Putting them in your business all the time
Where is the peace
Can't even sleep for trying to think
of ways to save my streets
What's the purpose? What's the cause?
There's plenty of reason
I need to know where is my freedom?

Court System

Here I am hands behind my back
Facing the judge in front of this oak
About to receive my time ten do five
I don't understand, but can't have nothing against this man
I did the crime now I have to do the time
These streets I need to leave it be
Cause it's not worth my time in the penitentiary
Family and friends crying, Cause I'm about to go down
Me out here trying to stay on my grind
I pray to god he gives me one more time
My family I should have been more serious about
Now I could be losing them all
 Because of my foolish mistake
I can't watch my kids grow into this place
My freedom this time I won't play with
So I won't have to face this court system
My family and friends I will be with them
Not some place far away
I promise to give my all
Cause I know no one love accepting collect calls.

Where Were You

You had me at birth I was one of your first,
How could you look me in my face and say not today?
When I'm the one trying to make an escape,
So we all can make a way, nice cars and a big house
Is what we want, more money, yes indeed it's what we need.
One hour of your time to push me to the line
Yet I felt like crying when you said not this time.
Look at me and say write baby girl write,
Then I can put a little speed to it.
So when my poems reach the hood
While all of you are hanging out
Realize that it was always something about this girl.
Sisters, brother, father and friends listened
And I thank all of you for your attention.
Mother don't look no further,
I'm going to show you who is smarter
Just like I showed my father.
When I make it to the top,
This here ain't gonna stop.
Mom, I know in my thoughts
The question to you will always be,
Where were you?

Part 5: My First Love: Toney

There he was standing by the cafeteria during lunch time at school. I was in the ninth grade at Long high. We both were staring at each other. Thank GOD that he had the nerve to approach me first. I was known as a tomboy. I didn't even think no guy at school would want to talk to me.

"What's going on Ms. Lady" is what he said to me.
"Not too much," I responded back to him.
"My name is Toney," he said.
"My name is Teisha," I said back.
"Look Teisha, I was wondering if I could invite you to lunch or maybe the movies one day?"
"I would love to go out with you Tony. When and where should we meet?"
"Baby I have a Trans Am. I can pick you up at your place Friday night at 6:30pm, if it's o.k with you."
"Sure Toney, I will call to give you my address later."

Toney and I had lots of fun together that Friday night. As the months went by, Toney and I started being intimate with one another. I became pregnant with our son Toney Jr.

Toney Jr. became the next love of my life. He was more than any gift that GOD could have ever given me. I love the way he smiled every time I talked to him in baby language. These were the kind of moments I wished I could remember from my mom. When I tickled his little toes, he had the craziest laugh that I ever heard. My life had just begun with a new family.

As the years went by, Toney became the kind of guy who

wanted me for himself. After a while, I saw that was not a good thing. He became a very violent person. The first time Toney became very violent we both were sitting in my living room area. The phone rang about 9 pm that night. Toney answered the phone and supposedly, on the other end, was a guy saying that he had the wrong number. For some reason, Toney did not believe this guy. I saw it in his eyes. At that time, my heart started to beat very fast - not knowing what was about to happen.

    I started walking toward my bedroom about to get some rest. I heard a clicking sound when I past Toney in our hall way. I then turned around to see Toney pointing a gun directly in my face. I started crying asking Toney

    "What's going on? Why are you pointing your gun in my face?"

    He yelled at me and said,

    "I was your first love and I will be your last" and then he pulled the trigger...

    At that time, my entire life flashed before my eyes. The gun wasn't loaded, but it might as well have been because I started having nightmares about how things would have been as if he did.

    In my first nightmare, *he shot me in the head. I then fell to the floor 5 steps away from my son. Everything started to look blurry. All I could see at this time was Toney walking near me. I could feel tears running down my face. I did not hate him for that. While he was walking near me, I saw flashes before me. I had a flash of him holding our son at the hospital. I had a flash of him making love to me. I even had a flash of us standing at the altar of my church home. With tears still running down my face, he stared at me and then walked past me. He came back and bent over so that my baby boy could kiss me goodbye on the fore head.*

    I couldn't say a sound. About 10 minutes passed and I'm still laying on my floor in my blood. I could hear about four hard knocks

at the door. I'm losing a lot of blood - almost out for the count. I thought I was in heaven when I saw bright lights shining in my eyes. Mam can you hear me? I slowly opened my eyes. All I saw was two people standing over me that looked like rescue workers. I felt the tears running down my face again.

"You're going to be just fine. can you hear me? Can you tell me who did this to you? If you can squeeze my hand one time for yes and two times for no."

I had to think about my baby and squeezed two times very slow. My head was hurting.

After leaving the E.R., I now have a room in the upper level of Grady Hospital on the 6th floor. The door opened, it was Toney and the baby. He was walking near me and my heart was racing again. I then pressed for the nurse. Toney saw me as I did that.

"If you tell anyone that I did this to you I promise I will kill you the next time." Toney whispered in my ear.

"How may I help you?" The sound that came from the intercom behind me.

"May I please have a cup of ice," I asked.

"Sure, someone will be right with you mam."

"Good girl, he said to me, kissing me on the fore head."

Can I please hold my son," I politely asked him.

"Yeah he is your son too. He has been crying all day. I think he misses you." Toney said.

"Here you go mam. Is there anything else I can do before leaving out? What's wrong with your eyes? Is something in it?" the nurse said to me.

Toney jumped up to see what I was doing.

"No mam, it was something from the baby clothes got into my eye, thank you that will be all for now."

"I guess you have a death wish," Toney said to me. I was hoping the nurse would know that my eyes were blinking at her to get help, but she didn't realize what I was doing.

Broken

"Toney, what are you saying baby, it's over now, let's please put this behind us. We have a child to raise"....And this is where I would wake up from the dream every time.

I had the same dream every night for about two weeks. After Toney put that gun in my face, things were just not the same for me. I became very scared of Toney. Everything he asked me to do I jumped and did it. Toney and I eventually became close again.. We started back doing things together as a family should. I saw that I still had strong love for Toney. I reminded myself that no one else cared about me. So I used that to get me through this relationship with him.

Toney ran everyone that did care about us out of our lives so neither of us had friends and barely a family. I knew my family wanted to help me, but I wouldn't let them.

Toney Jr. was now 3 years old. I think because Toney Jr. was older and much wiser, Toney hasn't been violent to me as often. He seemed to have at least that much respect for our son.

On January 1st, about 3am in the morning, Toney tried to kill me for real. I just knew this was going to be the last time that Toney would ever harm me again. I loved Toney so much that I accepted everything he had to issue me. It had gotten to that point that I didn't have any more room for him in my heart. He had made me a very unhappy person. I don't regret the child he gave me, but I do regret meeting him.

Toney had become so disrespectful to me. He started talking to other females in front of me. I didn't care; he had made me blind from the love that he planted inside me years ago. I gave Toney chance after chance, something my care taker forgot to teach me not to do. Maybe because she was busy being a fool in love also. It seemed that love was coming to tear me down so that it could build me up.

See, my relationship with Toney had become my darkest day and it stole my joy. I believe that Toney really and truly cared for me, but the kind of love he had for me, got dangerous to the point that I couldn't be with him anymore. Going through the process of breaking up with Toney caused me so many scary nights and lots of pain from hurt. I started thinking about the haunting nightmares of him shooting me, and him telling me over and over again that he would kill me. I started laughing every time Toney said those words. I thought that Toney was scared of going to jail, but he wasn't. On January 1st at about 3am new years day morning, Toney wanted to go out with his guy friend. He said to me in front of his guy friend "Bitch I'll be back". So I ran behind him trying to get my door key. I told him, "If you leave out my door, don't come back this way in the next year. You should be with your family in the New Year, how could you do this to us?"

All of a sudden, I built up the nerve to take my keys out of his hands. After I did that, Toney walked away. When he came back, I saw that he had a knife. The next thing I knew, he stabbed me in the back 4 times in and out with a steak knife. It hurt so badly. It felt like one went straight through my heart. Toney tried stabbing me in my chest also but I held on to his arm very tightly so that he couldn't. His guy friend was just standing there. I begged Toney's friend to please help me, but instead he rolled his eyes and walked away. I held on long enough to call for our son Toney Jr. because I knew he couldn't hurt me long as his son was around. Toney Jr. yelled out "no daddy please don't kill mommy."

Holding my head back just to see my son with his hands near his mouth to GOD

"don't let daddy kill my mommy."

After that, Toney looked down at me and said,

"Oh my GOD, what did I just do?"

Toney then left. I taught Toney Jr. how to call 911 and he did. I was told that I passed away, but when the ambulance got

Broken

to my place they saw Toney Jr. giving me mouth to mouth. I always played this game with him teaching him how to bring another person back to life. I never thought I would be his first patient. It was then and only then that I realized I really did love Toney enough to leave him before I decided to kill his ass because his death threats had almost come to pass.

After breaking up with Toney, he got with another woman and they had two kids together - a boy and a girl. He was taking her through the same thing he had taken me through. I talked to her from time to time for our kid's sake. We both found out that Toney was abused by his mother. Maybe he was punishing us for what his mom did to him. I also think that's why he couldn't be so violent in front of Toney Jr. He didn't want to pass those genes on. It was too late for the both of us to feel sorry for him. The other woman had more balls than me. I heard that she lit gasoline to Toney and then locked all the doors to their house so that he couldn't escape. That's the way he died.

My son asked about his dad all the time, I tell Toney Jr. that his dad is on a long vacation, and that he won't be back. But his dad always put him first and he will always love him.

I have time to think

I was that person at one time rude
By this man that called himself a real dude
Had no time to do anything
Only because he didn't won't me to be seen
Have friends I can count on my finger
He tried getting rid of them one by one
Until I said hell no it's time for you to go
Thought I would never say that line
But at that moment it was the right time
Time was moving very slow
I prayed that this would one day end
Knowing I was a real woman didn't want to be caught up in sin
Those promises he told me didn't mean a thing
To him it was just something to do
Please don't let your blind side
Get you caught up in this shit to
To you I will always love you
But it's time for me to move on
And be with the one I truly belong
I'm taken my joy back
Remember it's the one you use
To stab me in the back
Thank god for wakin' me up
Showing me what was really for me
And most for giving me time to think

Made it Out

You brought me down when I thought we were all we had,
So sad you have now made me mad.
When I look at you I want to say kiss my ass.
You had me crying; I felt like dying.
Now part two of my life,
I'm a wife how nice;
Last I heard your girl wasn't treating you right.
That's a crying shame now tell me whose the blame,
Don't want to know hope she don't drive you insane.
You cheated, lied, and misused me; knowing all those things were wrong,
But they all made me strong,
Now I can say it's time to move on.

Lateisha Varner

Do You Know Me

You thought I was dumb, you claimed the love we had was the best.
Until you got the big head, running the streets,
Having fun with friends, and staying away from home;
Has caused me to move on; however,
I kept pretending the love was still there.
You caused more pain to my heart. I gave you my life.
Told you things I never told before,
Thanks, that's what kept you in my door.

Knowing I have a fear of being alone
Each day I pray that God takes that away.
So I just keep lusting for you as if I'm happy,
Happy as ever before and when you touch me
I show you signs I'm not afraid.
When you love me I show you this will never end.
When we talk I show you I'm listening.
But if you only knew, I'm not paying none of that any attention.
You have scarred my heart even more.
Now I need a new one, so I won't tear the next love apart.

Sleeveless

Sleeveless boy, sleeveless boy
What you doing down there in that small place?
Say you want me to come close
So you can see what it feels like to touch the girl next door.
Sleeveless boy stop that!
You know my mom is not going to let you put a foot on her floor,
So pick up your bags and go home,
Trying to prove you are strong.
Sleeveless boy it won't be long
Till we are on our own
Sleeveless boy I hope you are right
You are the one I can call my own.

Part 6: My Second Love: Joe

Joe was something special to me. I had never met anyone like him before. I was staying in this subdivision called Power Place Forrest. This was a very small subdivision. There were made like apartments to me. Everybody knew everybody out there. This is where I met Joe. There was a block party going on in my subdivision. I will never forget that day. It was April 10, 1999. Joe's cousin was throwing him a party because he was just released from prison. He was just sittin' there in a white chair drinking on some Zima.

"Hey Tim," I yelled out to Joe's cousin.

"What crazy girl. Can't you see me over here trying to finish cooking?"

They all called me crazy girl because they say I had 2 lives to live. I had a little anger inside me also. I would yell and scream at people for no reason.

"Tim set me up with your cousin Joe," I asked him.

"Teisha, girl you and Joe would be another Bonnie and Clyde and we don't need that in this subdivision."

I didn't care. I was damaged on the inside anyhow.

"Damn Tim. Who is this fine girl?" Joe said in a gansta way?

Then I turned around and said "who me? Who do you want me to be," In a thug girl way.

"My new girl hopefully, but I know you can't handle a thug like me," Joe said.

Broken

"Nigga please! I can't handle what? You ain't said nothing but a word."

"So what's up." Joe said.

"O.k. then. I guess this mean that I'm your girl now. Let me warm you, once you fall deep into me there's no return. I heard through the grape vine that I'm a very dangerous person. My soul is now like lighting. You'll never know when or where I will strike."

So it was then that Joe and I became girlfriend and boyfriend. I heard that he had a baby mother. So what, she wasn't with him then.

"All hell is going to open up now," Tim said to everyone laughing out loud.

"Ha,ha stop laughing Tim. I don't want your cousin Joe to think that I am crazy."

"Shit, you is and you know that."

At that moment, I felt like lighting and he was water. We were ready to spark fire. From what I heard, he was dangerous also.

"Whatever cuz. Me and Teisha is about to take a walk so that we can get to know each other a litter better."

"Just make sure yall come back before the party ends."

"alright cuz. We'll be right back."

Joe and I had so much in common almost. The only thing we didn't have in common was him always going back and forth to jail. I got so tired of that shit. Every time I was right at that point of giving him my all, there he was going back to jail. The last time Joe got out of jail was February 4, 2000. We made love like there was going to be no tomorrow.

"Get your ass up!" He yelled out loud while I was still asleep. For a moment, I thought that Toney had come back from the dead so I jumped up and it was Joe, the love of my life.

"Quiet Joe, my son is still asleep. Why are you yelling at me anyway baby what's wrong?"

"Who in the hell was you fucking with while I was in jail?"

"No one. What are you talking about baby? Please, I can't take going through nothing like this anymore Joe. Please tell me what's wrong. I'm scared baby. Please don't try and fight me while my son is in the next room or ever. If you can't trust me, sorry to say, but my son and I will have to leave. I been through this before. I have my son and I promised him that I wouldn't take him through that again. My son and I live on trust and promises that will never be broken. So it's your decision. I love you. I have since the day I met you. You are the only one that has my heart other than god and my son. My clit has room only for your dick. Anyway, you got these niggas scared to say hello to me. Come on. Have you forgotten you're water and I'm lighting. I don't know one person that will play with fire."

"I'm sorry Teisha. I just love you so much, and I'm scared that you may choose someone else over me because of my stupid ass mistake."

"Joe, you know that I will never do nothing like that. We are a family. You and Lil Toney is all I have now. I love you so much Joe. I don't even think 1000 words could explain how I feel about you now."

"O.K. baby, again I'm sorry. I need for you to get ready. I'm about to meet Anthony at his house."

"Joe, I hope that you are not about to buy none of that bull shit that make you go crazy. Let me get Lil Toney ready so that we can stop him by my mom's house first."

When I got with Joe, I never knew about his drug addiction. Once I found out, I was already in love with him. His drug addiction, my friends, or family members could not stop how I felt about Joe. I'm glad that I wasn't weak to join him in his world of peace. Whatever drugs he was on, it made him nice to me, but mean to everybody else.

Drugs sometime made Joe beat and say crazy things to me that I know he didn't mean. Joe made me feel like I was in another world. It was something different about my life all of a sudden. I couldn't control it anymore. My son loved him so much that he didn't see the bad in Joe. He thought Joe was his dad. I thought raising my son would change his ways, but it didn't. One day, I decided to see what had Joe so strong out. I really can't remember which one of Joe's friends let me have a taste of powder, which is a form of cocaine. After Joe walked out the room to do whatever he had came to do, that's when it all happened. Joe never did drugs around me, not even after I found out. Once Joe found out about me trying it that day, he kicked my ass, and said, "This isn't you. It's for people that don't give a damn about their self, or feel like they are here alone. You have no reason because you have me. I'm never going to leave you." That's when I knew how much he really cared about me. So I never did it again.

On June 5, 2000, I found out Joe and I were having a baby. We both were very excited. We started shopping for baby clothes and toys. Until this one day, I called for him up at his grandmother house and Joe wasn't there. I waited days to hear from Joe, but he never called so I just left it alone. I knew then that me and my son, Lil Toney, were going to have a long summer. Joe was like a thug in a child's body. So many people loved him and so many hated him. He was just that kind of guy that no one understood. Joe had done so much to hurt people. I really don't think he meant to do any of it. Joe was looking for attention, but in the wrong way.

I heard Joe went back to this female who was known as a Gold Digging Hoe. Joe had told me about this female a while back during the time when he was incarcerated. When Joe got out of jail, this female started coming around more than usual. I knew that something wasn't right about that picture then, but Joe insisted that I was tripping. I guess she wanted to make sure Joe didn't forget her. Maybe because she saw how much he cared about me. Some of us know how dirty females can be. And not only that, Joe was the kind of man to die for.

I finally had a chance to get in touch with him. I called him at his grandmom's house.

"Hello, may I speak with Joe please."

"Joe isn't here is this Teisha?"

"Yes this is Teisha who is this?"

"You already know sweetie. Look, Joe and I are now together. You no longer exist."

"Bitch what?"

Let's not forget that I'm four months pregnant at the time. I felt like I had open heart surgery. The doctor had poured gasoline on my heart, stitched me up, and lit a match down my throat. I felt like I was on fire. Like the devil I wanted to drag her ass to hell.

To hear her laugh while telling me this, I could have snatched her ass through the phone. There are six things in my life I don't play about, all jokes aside; 1, my god, 2, my child, 3, my family, 4, my man, 5, my money, and last, the only thing that's keeping me from killing this hoe - my fragile heart. While crying, I could hear Joe in the back ground telling me not to believe what she was saying. But still, what was she doing over there and where have you been, I asked him.

Joe was on house arrest. He wasn't allowed to leave within 30 feet of his home. He should have still informed me about his relationship with her.

Joe took someone's car that night so that he could come and explain all of this to me. He heard it in my voice that I was lost. I didn't want to hear anything he had to say. My son depended on him to be a father and I needed him to be my future husband. I didn't want to see him ever again in life. I was numb. He didn't exist anymore. Joe allowed this whore to trash our dreams. In my mind, I'm telling myself never to fall in love again cause the next are going to do the same thing. All I can say now is sorry for the next man. Let me put that in a she devil attitude.

Five months later, after he left me, I got a phone call from him on November 11, 2000 about 4:35pm. He wanted me to know that he was sorry for causing me emotional stress, and that he wanted to make up for it all. I accepted Joe's apologies. But never could I have given him my heart again. He explained that he was calling from this female's mom's house and not to call it back only because he didn't want no mess between she and I. I welcomed karma into my heart and call the bitch house anyway. Now I wonder how my venom taste in her mouth. They say give your hater a taste of your special made medicine every now and then. I was going to cause her to leave him the same way he did me. And to show her that it wasn't her pussy, it was her money. I heard nothing else from him after that.

The next day, which was November 12, 2000, my water broken and I was having real bad contractions. I remember calling out for Joe. I needed him at this time. I was scared. I got a visit from my mom at the hospital just to tell me that Joe was murdered. She was told that Joe was trying to rob someone. I was thinking how ironic, my son's birth and his father's death. If I'm not mistaken, it all happened seven minutes apart. GOD must have been jealous of something I was doing because he was taking everybody I cared about out my life. At this time, I didn't even know if I should show my kids love. It seemed that everyone who cared for me was gone. The thing that hurts me the most about Joe being gone is I had the nerve to tell him that I didn't love him anymore after talking to him the day before.

The truth, I really did still love him so deeply I can't even explain that feeling. He was the next best thing in my life after

Tina. If I would have known GOD was going to take him I would've said to him," Yes I do still love you." But I thank God for not letting him leave before telling me goodbye. So you see, I want to tell this Gold Digging female no thanks for making my life sadder; but thanks for making me more of a woman. Just in case you thought you were hurting me. See, you did me and him a favor. You helped put him in a better place so that he doesn't have to try so hard for attention anymore. As for me, you made me a strong survivor. Again, we thank you; Me, Joe, and his son.

    Three days after Joe's death was his home coming. I was in the hospital. After I was released from the hospital with our son, I notice that there was something hanging out of me. I called 911, when the ambulance got to my place they knew what it was after seeing it hanging from below me. They asked if I had just had a baby? I then said yes. They said it looked as if my after birth was still inside me. For sure it was after hearing it from the E.R. nurse. She also stated the sack was also left inside me. They said they didn't see how I made it three days with all that mess left inside me. They had to drug me with medication because the work that was about to be done was going to be painful to me. After they drugged me up, I started dozing off, but I could hear them saying that I was losing a lot of blood. I then saw more doctors coming in the room. I felt tears running down my face cause out of all these years, I prayed on my life to be taken and to be closer to GOD, it was now my time. Fighting to keep my eyes open, I prayed one last prayer on my life. I asked GOD to spare me so that I could be a mother to my kids - something I didn't have. I didn't want them to go through what I went through without me being here to protect them. And indeed, he spared my life. From all this I learned that no man shall serve two master, for he will hate one and love the other.

Cheater

You snooze you lose! It was you that played yourself like a fool.
You played me once, you played me twice,
when I was the one, giving you positive advice.
I let you in, you let yourself out she creeps you in
You're such an ass now you're on the couch.
Come back, Hmmm, I wish I would… what you can do
is take yourself back to the hood.
Now run and tell your boys that.
Because, I'm certain you won't be back.
Yes, my heart may burn, knowing you chose her over me;
can't be from lack of love that I gave you too much of
Did you love her because she was high red?
So what was I, that you couldn't have loved me instead?
See she made you very blind to true love.
I tried my best to love you, but couldn't.
Your foolishness had you staying out late.
Now Pattie cake, Pattie cake, I knew I saw a rattle snake
What you didn't know, is that years ago
I put your stuff in the closet, next to the front door.
My love you have lost.
Can this be her gain? Have you asked yourself?
Will this make me insane?
After all the years we gained.
Now get up, and get out,
I never thought that would come from my mouth.
It's all over. No tossing and turning, hearts not burning.
Finally, I can sit back and enjoy my journey.

One Night Stand

Feeling so empty inside, trying to find my happiness
Wishing that cool breeze brush against my skin
To chill the flame of fire from within
See love casted me down to hell
Trying to pay you back for shit you could not reveal
Stay back five feet, don't think you can handle
What just became of me
My memories will not allow me
To forget your gentle touch
The smell of your cologne
That lies on my private parts
During the time we thought was love
But at the end it was nothing but pure lust
Bending me over didn't put out the flame
Whispering in my ears really made you more of the blame
Five feet I said before you make me insane
My name is naw
Something I should've said
When you cause me to step outside my vows
That pleasure from the other night
Yes got me very crunked
But not at all did it cause me
To forget him not even once
It did change my life for better
So hey man think you for that one night stand
I place this in my book
Under my stormy weather

You Left

Still trying and understand what could've went wrong
Couldn't been so badly you had to leave me alone
Twice I refuse to let you do me wrong
You said you loved me but still had the strength
To walk out my door
I cried for days waiting and waiting
Praying you would come back but never did
I had nothing else to do but think of you
Not realizing I was being a fool in love
Look at me now I'm so cool
Take a look in your mirror now who's the fool
Time is passing by losing control trying to make sacrifice
I'm wasting my time and losing my mind
Seeking for help when there's no one to find
You left me all alone
Crying and hurting, running and searching, hoping and praying
But it's all okay I still made it to the top
And all my thanks goes out to you my love
But you can never come back no you'll never be back.

Liar

Happy but can't smile,
Sound strange but real,
You have taken it all.
The joy you gave
The love you put in me
Mostly the care that none could get.
Now I have accepted your unknown lies.
While the inside of me is bursting with flame of fire.
My heart has been torn by this so called desire of mine.
The smart one I will choose to be
And not let you take what's left of me.

It Aint Easy

Stay clear of me I'm a little girl trying to break free.
Move out my way so I can say what I have to say.
Open my mouth let him hear me out.
Tell him a onetime broken heart,
It ain't easy.
To pull apart during the second go round
No it ain't easy.
Looking with a stare you are right
It's something you wouldn't want to bare
That's why out my mouth I never say swear
Looking up, I guess this is what they call fair.
You are my angel, my angel above the sky,
Wishing you could wipe my tears when I cry.
How long will the hurt last?
Not yet letting go of the past.
That's why I have to open my mouth.
Tell him that a onetime broken heart.
It ain't easy,
To pull apart during the second go round.

Walking Out Her Life

Why walk out on someone as lovely as sparking stars?
Lonely she doesn't like to be, but for the one she truly loves she can accept even if it hurts
He won't know about that since he's not the one hurting
After hurting for love it feels like eternity
Years have gone pass, still no love, turn around and still emptiness.
So you ask again, does he love me?
How would they know?
When their heart is full of joy and yours is crashing down
So wipe your tears, hide your fears keep going with the years.
Come here! Ask me; just leave it be.

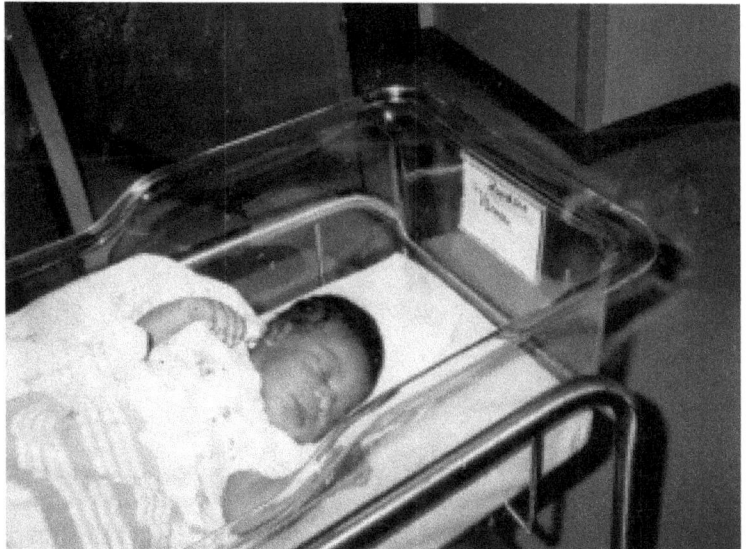

This is when the doctor brought baby Joe into my room for the first time. I'd just waken up from the sleeping pills they had me on.

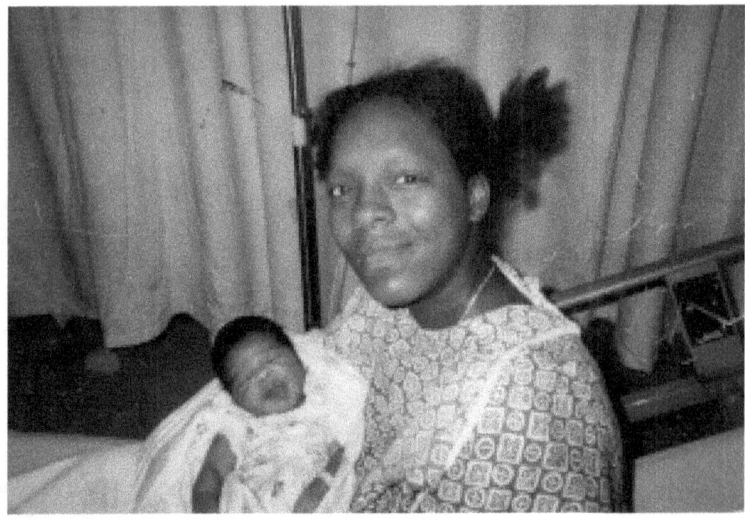

I don't know what kind of medicine they had me on at the hospital to keep my mind off of Joe Jr's father's death, but I wasn't happy at all.

Broken

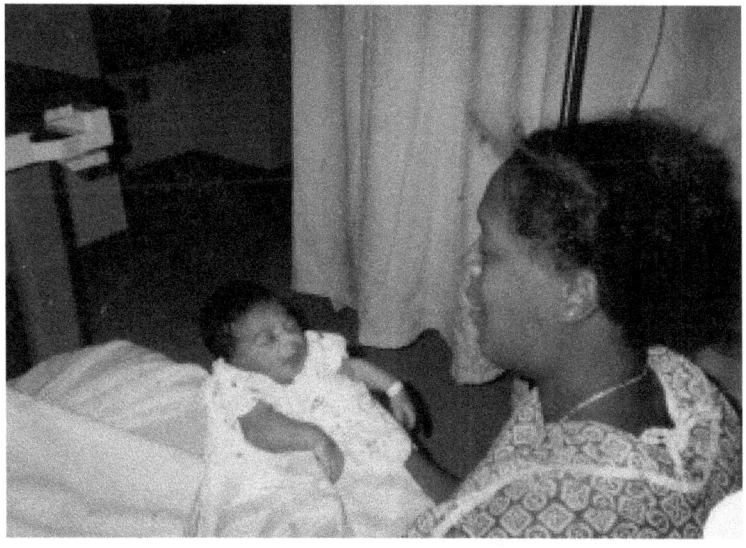

I just couldn't stop looking at him. Why couldn't Joe be here to enjoy this moment with me.

Lateisha Varner

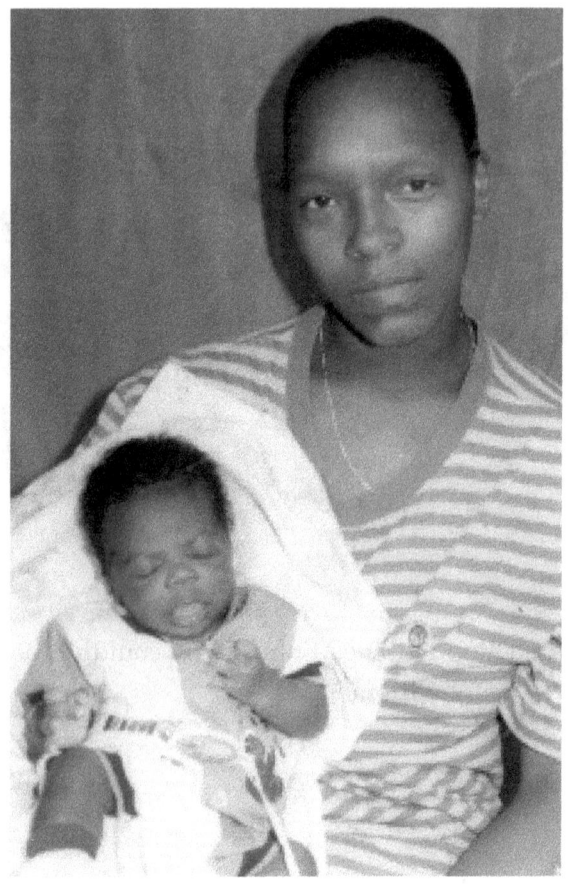

This picture was taken a week after I came from the hospital. I'm still feeling sad.

Part 7: *The Man I Prayed For*

I stepped out on faith and moved to Decatur Georgia with a family member not bring there with me. I didn't know my way around Decatur. I hit I-20 east doing about 80 mph. I was trying to make sure no one was following me so that I couldn't be talked out of moving from Atlanta, the land of pain, but I knew no one was going to do that - not for little ole me.

Once I found a place to stay, I stayed in the house for a while. I didn't want me and my 2 boys to get to know anyone. So we were never seen by anyone. I was on food stamps assistance. When I moved to Decatur, my food stamp file was lost in the Department of Family and Children Services warehouse area. So now I had to leave out the house to find out what was going on with my case. Every time I had to leave my apartment to take care of important business, there was this boy who stayed in the apartment under mine always singing this rap song called "Help Me to Change My Ways". I used to frown every time he sang that song because in my mind, I was wondering who was going to help me change my ways..

One day, he approached me and asked for my name. I told him Teisha. He then said his name was Jay. I said "okay Jay what's up? I'm busy, I have business to take care of."

"Why are you so stuck up?" He asked me.

I said "What? You don't even know me. How are you going to call me stuck up?"

"I don't mean no harm. I was just trying to make conversation Ms. Lady," he said.

"I'm sorry Jay. I'm just going through something right now."

"Can I say if you need someone to talk to you can come down stairs and talk to me."

I told him that sounded okay because I needed someone to show me around Decatur anyway.

"Can I ask you a personal question?"

"Sure what's on your mind?" Jay asked.

"Do I look like I need a man?"

"No."

"Well, is it because you see me with two boys and no dads?"

"No."

"So tell me what do you see in me?"

"I know someone made you bitter. And I can see pain in your eyes. Help me to change my ways isn't for me. It's from me to you."

"Sound like I keep hearing those same lines over and over every time I see a guy. See you later. I have to go. I'm sorry for my rudeness."

"Hey Teisha, he yelled out while I was walking to the bus stop.

"Yeah, what's up Jay?"

"I was wondering if I could play football with the kids one day."

"Sure," I said, "long as it's in the front yard."

"How about tomorrow?" he said.

"That would be perfect. I'll have them ready."

The next day came Jay knocked on my door and asked for the kids. I gave him their names the day before. My kids were very happy to be going outside. Going down the stairs there Jay was singing that song "Help Me to Change My Ways." I admit, it was kind of cute. I knew that song was for me to notice. How was

Broken

I supposed to help him change his ways and how was he going to help me with mine. I wasn't ready to move on into another relationship. Jay has now brought the kids back into the house.

"Thank you so much Jay. I really needed that break."

"Where's the father? Is he in their life because I don't want to cause no problem."

"You already have, my kids love you," I said blushing at him.

"Well, Lil- Toney father is decease. So is little Joe's. Both of their father's were murdered."

"I'm sorry to hear that." Jay sadly said to me.

"That's okay, I need someone to talk to cause sometime I think I'm going crazy. But I have to hold up for my kids' sake."

"I can play step dad if you want me too. I don't have kids of my own and I'm also single."

Screaming to myself, "God stop this madness. I can't take going through this again."

"Slow down, let's get to know each other first before talking about being their step dad." I said to Jay.

Months later Jay and I ended up in a relationship. I thought Joe was the best I ever had. Joe didn't have shit on Jay. Jay knew how to role play like he belonged in a holly wood porn and I was his freak. I didn't know how flexible I was until he had me bending all kind of ways like a slinky. The way he touch me was so soft, the way he loved me was so gentle, and the way he talked to me was not so commanding. I thought God had made me a little girl again. I was happy all over. This man made me feel so alive. He became more of a father to my kids. I was proud to have met him, but after a couple of years into our relationship, he started to act like the rest. He wasn't the man I met in the beginning anymore. He started selling drugs and claimed that it was to support the house. He started going in and out of jail more and more. I was getting lonely and my kids were beginning to feel fatherless again.

After he got out, he asked me to marry him. No one ever asked me that so I knew that he was serious. He promised that if I said yes, he will never sell drugs again.

Six years went by very fast. The man I prayed for and I were still close friends. He had not been back in the streets. The friends he had all disappeared, but that didn't stop the man of my life from loving me. I gave him his first child on October 1 2006. That really gave him a chance to be more of a man. Even though six years had gone by, I would still sit and cry about Joe's death.

He watches me over and over tearing myself down about this. I thank God that he respects the fact that Joe was once the love of my life, and he was taken from me while I was having our son. Jay has been so supportive. I some time sit in my living area lighting candles, drinking beer, listening to sad songs, while looking at the picture of Joe. He then gets the kids and take a walk or something. He said that's the time I need to be alone. Shedding tears may help me to overcome his death. Today, the pain and the cries still live in me. I don't think it will ever leave as long as I live, and have to face what he left behind - his child.

Four more years had gone by, and we had been together for ten years. He now has a job as a construction worker. He still hasn't gone back to the streets. On November 4, 2009, I gave him his second child. He was born on Election Day. The baby's middle name is Obama. He is a hand full. The man I prayed for deserves both his kids. He became a dad before his time and I thank him for it. Today we are still close and I love him dearly.

Vows

My vows to you my love
Will explain it all
When we walk down the aisle;
We are one of a kind
You best believe we won't part,
Till someone tells us we are dying.
Everything about you makes my world shine.
I hop, you hop, the love we have will never stop.
Joy you gave me, happiness you placed inside me,
Thank you for bringing me to society.
Just when I thought every part had died within me,
You made me believe,
When I thought I couldn't achieve.
It's because of you now I can stand.
Again, I thank God that you are my man.
You are my one in all.
That's the reason I wrote these vows.

My Hands

Dad you are my pal I cannot stay, so please give me away.
I have a man that wants my hands,
All those years of playing in the sand was the best
When I was too young to have a man;
I have to go, so please allow me to leave your door.
I love you Dad, don't look so sad
Because I'm going to be glad
He is my heart; he is part of my soul.
He made me his, now we have to grow old
He promised to love me, and only me
On the alter he will say I do only GOD knows if it's true
He will place the ring while I shed tears of joy
That is the moment I have patiently waited for
A woman you have made me out to be
I'll never forget your funny jokes
Hearing you tell me how beautiful I am
So please don't be sad because in the end you are still my dad.

Step dad

Thinks for loving me
And taking on my responsibility
The way my dad should had
And for loving my mom
During the time she was sad
You turned out to be more
Of a dad than I expected
You taught me most of what I know
All my dad should've showed
My mom trusted our life in your hands
You did more than what you had
To prove that you was a real man
I think god for chosen our house for you to stand
I know it was much to bear
But I will never go without saying
Think you for being there

Part 8: My Kids

I made a promise to GOD when I got older that if he granted me kids, I promise to love them all the days of my life. My four boys mean the world to me. They are the cure that is my survival. My boys really never left my side because I didn't want the world to disappoint them like it did me. So they were always around every time I got high. It seemed as if that's when they showed me the most love. I believe they knew I needed to be loved.

To be so young, they knew more about me than my sisters and brother. I taught my kids very well to love one another and to never turn their backs on each other no matter what happens - just in case GOD decided to take me home while they were still young. GOD can take me now and I truly believe that they can do all this without help from anyone.

My kids and I are a team. We do so much together. We all have our days from time to time, but there's nothing too serious that it can destroy the love we have for one another.

My Precious Gift

God has place someone so wonderful and precious in my life,
Holding him makes me feel so thankful for this day.
One to ten little fingers wiggling like growing vines,
One to ten little toes that will one day catch up with mine.
You are so small I'm here to protect you,
This world has no clue how much I thank God for giving me you.
This precious little one I look down at with a wide smile,
Yes it is my God given child.

Desire

God gave you to me, and I took you away,
Even when I tried I couldn't go another day.
I prayed to God my soul to take,
In that other world he gives me a chance to see your face.
Many tears I shared,
Each drop proved I really cared.
Holding my belly knowing there's nothing to bear,
It's just the thought of knowing you were there.
In my dreams is when we play,
So let's sleep until another day.

My Child

Weather I had one, two, three, maybe more
You were given to me as a gift. Look at you
I want to cherish you only if
I can love you until
You're every movement I won't waste
I will be here for you
Believe what I say you're my child
That I don't want to miss
Not one day

Part 9: *Allowing God to Take Over*

    I can't remember exactly what I was going through. All I could remember was getting high. I got so high I even cashed in the money order for my rent, which was about four hundred dollars. It was about 3am in the morning. Of course I wasn't the only one gettin high. I was on low income housing at the time. I didn't have too many bills; I guess that's why I did stupid things. I didn't let too many people know about my short term addition because I knew it would hurt them, so I kept it from most people. That day I spent and I spent. The dope man didn't even want to serve us anymore. In a way, I was kind of glad my body knew it couldn't take anymore drugs in, but the feeling just felt too good.

    I was trying to call the drug dealer again and again but the phone did not have a dial tone anymore. It had a sound of wind in the receiver. That took me back to when I was a litter girl. My mom and dad were still together at this time. We had this funny looking phone. Nobody in my house ever used this phone. Until one day, I decided to talk on the phone. Out of nowhere I heard the sound of wind - like it was coming from far away. Then, I heard a voice say Teisha come on I'm right here. I was really scared cause the voice sounded like the JESUS I saw on TV. I threw the phone on the floor and waited a couple of days before picking it back up.

    When I picked the phone up for the second time, I promise you it was always that same voice. I had gotten used to talking to JESUS. I wish I could remember what it was we always talked about. Maybe it wasn't for me to remember. I think that I was one of the ones that he came to at an early age to let me know that he will always be near, and not to worry because he will be the one to carry me out. He knew at the age of 32 years old that I was still going to be a child in an adult body. - still searching for a mother and a father. I wanted to die because I heard that Mary was a good mother to JESUS, therefore, JESUS would have been my brother. I wondered if JESUS was my brother would my dad have given me the same powers. It's a good thing that I wasn't because I would have used my power for all the wrong reasons. And I would have known that my dad and brother did not like ugly.

Looking back at all that, I still wanted more drugs. While riding around looking for them, my mind kept telling me that I was fine go ahead keep on driving. I think that JESUS was in the passenger seat. He showed me that I was going 10mph. The devil in the back seat telling me to keep going 10mph lets go get high. As I continued to drive at 10mph, I remembered seeing lights. It looked like I was entering the center of a circus. I could hear the person I was with call out my name.

"Teisha, stay with me please? Pull over before we crash into something."

The devil had a big hold over me at that time.

I had nothing on my mind, but to get high. The next day, it was rent time. I didn't have a dime for the rent man. I felt so badly about that so I pretended my job had shortened my paycheck, so he gave me two weeks to have the money.

I think after my high went down, something came over me. On Sunday, I went to this church called Pilgrim. When I walked through the parking lot of the church ground, God had already sent a message through the doors of the church before I even walked in. It was a feeling of guilt and shame that went flowing though my body. As service went on, I decided to get baptized. It felt good being born again - knowing that God has forgiven me of all my sins. I could hear the song "Never Seen the Righteousness Forsaken, by Bishop Eddie Long in my ears.

Broken

I kept going to church for a while, but we all know how fast the enemy can distract us when we are trying to turn our lives around. I didn't let him take over this time. I fought him with belief and faith. I had to do this alone - trying to hide what I had just run from. It was better that way. I had to get myself together for the sake of my kids. They didn't have anyone if they didn't have me so I did what I had to do. It felt good being who I was raised to be - a Christian girl. I started back writing and taking my kids out more often. During my recovery, I decided to write a book on my life - just a brief story on what I have been through now that there's nothing standing in my way.

I did start on my book and I got close to God. Everything about and around me started to change. I started losing the weight I didn't need any more. My nails and hair started growing. I had a glow about me. I was able to stand straight and not lean anymore. I just felt so alive. Each morning while taking my kids and husband to school and work, I listened to the Yolanda Adams inspiration morning show and Cocoa brother. It was everyday they had a word for me. I cried every time they came on because the feeling that was inside me was so strong. It was as if God was lifting all those tons of pain and hurt off of me. I thank the man upstairs for doing what he said he would do......He handled my battle.....PS. My mom and I are closer than ever now and I will love her till the end of my life.

Surrender

Looking up asking is today my day?
No answer.
Guess I have to sit back and wait.
I prayed today would be a new day,
Since I decided not to stray!
Look at me what do you see?
I know, a little girl in misery,
But has plenty of fantasy.
One writes songs and become like Akon,
A brother that has real peace where he's from
Love Rosa Parks and give a seat to a person just leaving dialysis.
Put that mess down, pour that crap out
This isn't what life is all about, ask the dead!
They'll tell you soon the lights will go out.
I'm walking to change because this here is a shame,
Don't point your fingers at me, this is what they call
Someone has made me insane.

Prayer

Finally, I stood up and said a prayer,
Really didn't think if anyone would care
But when looking around everyone had a tear to share.
Then I knew I was home, a home where no one is left alone.
Need help there's the door now you take the next step.
Need a hand there's the man that knows the plan.
In need of prayer, open your arms and he'll be there.
Trust in Thee and you to will see
Here is where you need to be.
So I said a prayer, a prayer that made a change in me.

Traveler

I wish I could fly looking up while the plane goes above the sky
All the crashing and bombings let's choose wisely for this seat
So we can get someone more responsible in Washington D.C.
They can fix it up or look at it twice
Still there's a man around the corner trying to plant a device.
Think I need to stay on ground even though their all around.
Babies crying, mother's praying, Stewards trying to keep everyone still
While the pilots keep hold of the wheel.
Everybody stops and pray it won't be this plane today.

Refrigerator

Please close your door
Don't want to see you anymore
Holding all I think I need
Lose your power get hot
So I won't grab that steak tonight
So temping looking at that left over mac and cheese
Please stop got to close your door
Can't take this craving anymore
O my GOD there's a coke
It will quench my thirst
I have to lose this weight
O hell I'm going to get that mac and cheese, get that coke
Grab that good ole steak and sit here with my plate
I just won't eat too late.

Lateisha Varner

School

Get smart, stay smart, you must read, read, and read
In the future your educational knowledge is what you need
Education first, family second, and friends last
At the end they will be glad you passed
School lunch gives you strength
That school bell gets you to class
Your school books give you knowledge
So that you can make it to college
Want to play games, want to be the prettiest, trying to be hard
Stop before you find yourself in that grave or maybe that jail cage
Save it
Beauty is nice, being hard is o.k. however
Let's not forget you'll here to make it
Your mothers send you off
Your teachers teach you
So what role do you play?
Do you play the role of not listening?
Or do you play the role of not paying attention?
Not trying to get in school suspension
Then you won't make it home to eat them good ole
Collards, yams, and fried chicken
I know you to need to listen and pay attention
And try not to get in school suspension

Tree Branch

If my arms stretched as long as yours
I would reach out for all those
That was in need for anything
Other than silver and gold
If I was your leaves I wouldn't fall
If each one stood for love
I would make sure I had enough for
Not one, not two, but all.
The ground I rest on would be a place for peace
There's plenty of room for someone like you and me
I'm here, not lost, but have nowhere else to go
Other than that each day I watch this world
Grow and grow
If I was a tree branch
I would stay strong
So that you would always
Have something to lean on

Lateisha Varner

*In Memory of
Sara Stone, Gerald Sr., Gerald Jr., Mary Varner*

About the Author

Born in Atlanta Georgia to Mr & Mrs Vivian & Oliver Varner, Lateisha Varner now resides in Decatur Georgia and spends her current days taking care of her family and writing books for little children. Praying that God will keep her lifted up, it is her hope that her books will keep smiles on countless little faces. Her goal is to bring hope and peace to those who feel lost. Stay tuned for all that is to come.

Upcoming Children's Books:
Let's Learn Colors and Numbers
Tooth Fairy
Getten Things Done Together

For book signings, contact:
vlateisha@ymail.com
www.authorLvarner.com

Thanks for your purchase. To redeem your CD, fill out this form, cut it out and send it to the address below.

```
Name: _____

Address: _____

         _____

Phone: _____

Email: _____

Place of Purchase: _____
```

Send form to:

South City Books

Attn: Author L. Varner's CD

P.O. Box 161311 Atlanta, GA 30321

South City Books
P.O. Box 161311 Atlanta, GA 30321

South City Books,
a rod hollimon company

www.southcitybooks.com

www.ingramcontent.com/pod-product-compliance
Lightning Source LLC
Chambersburg PA
CBHW071154090426
42736CB00012B/2336